LOOK UP!

Space Discoveries Prophesy

MELINDA FERRARI

Copyright © 2022 by Melinda Ferrari

Printed in the United States of America

ISBN 978-0-9754799-2-6

https://CampShineOut.Com

Dedication

This book is dedicated to the purpose for which it was created

iv

Table of Contents

Acknowledgement viii

Preface ....…............ix

Introduction................................…..........11

Cosmic Nature Walk 13

To Move or Not to Move..............…..........25

Space Travel Today in the Bible ....…....35

The Real Shape of the Earth 43

The Age of the Earth...................…..............49

Escaping Earth's Gravity 57

Why is the Universe Expanding ....…....63

Questions and Answers about Extraterrestrial......69

Amazing Benefits of Space Exploration............83

Manhattanhenge......................................91

Revelation's Happy Ending..................…......95

Space Sounds..................................……....……107

Conclusion ....…..113

About the Author ....…....…….115

Bibliography ....………..…….117

Acknowledgement

I wish to personally thank Dr Neil DeGrasse Tyson, astrophysicist, science communicator and host of the podcast StarTalk for his contribution to my inspiration in creating this book.

In addition, I wish to thank the following organizations and individuals for research material that they made available: National Aeronautics and Space Administration (NASA), National Geographic, The History Channel, Arjun Kharpal, et al.

Most importantly, I am grateful to the Creator for allowing me the noble privilege of learning more about his majestic universe.

Preface

Whatever the end-time prediction, apocalyptic or pleasant, space and space exploration will play a key role, and the result will be of cosmic proportions.

Never has the world witnessed a time of such elevated levels of prosperity, knowledge, and social networking as it presently does. All of this comes, mostly, because of space exploration, and this signals the immense future impact that space and its discoveries will have on our lives.

This book presents a wealth of information about space adventures and biblical predictions working in tandem to alert humanity about future events. The book is comprised of twelve essays that I wrote in response to information that I gleaned from science talks, debates, discussions, and publications. Each essay explains at least one space discovery and its significance to end-time prophecies, according to biblical writings and certain secular records. Additionally, I share some deep thoughts and ask several pertinent questions.

I consider it a privilege to share this work, *Look Up! Space Discoveries Prophesy,* with you, and I assure you that it will be an amazing revelation.

Introduction

The coronavirus pandemic lockdown of 2020 provided a respite from my regular work activities of teaching school. With reduced workload of fewer lessons to plan, tests to write and other such teacher-related responsibilities, I found myself immersed into watching science videos and reading publications about the cosmos, so much that I started to take notes.

As I watched and read, I realized the connection between these science topics and biblical information. As I continued learning more about space, I observed that space discoveries have led to more questions than answers, erupting in discussions and debates about the universe in which we reside. In my view, these discussions, and debates, though useful, seem to overshadow the real purpose of space exploration and its significance to the end time.

Considering this, I started to write about the specific role that space exploration is scheduled to play in the end of the world as we know it. The inspiration was divine; hence, I continued to research and learn. Consequently, I organized my thoughts into this book.

Now just a suggestion, as you explore these pages, pay attention to the trails of nuggets throughout. Follow them. They will eventually help to beam more light on space exploration and end-time prophecies.

It is my desire that every reader discovers in these pages something that brings him or her a deeper understanding, or awareness, of the matter discussed. Additionally, I hope to activate in each reader the desire to learn more about space exploration and end-time prophecies.

Chapter One

Cosmic Nature Walk

When I was a teenager, I belonged to a youth group that sometimes took its members on nature walks. We visited fields, orchards, botanical gardens, pastures, homes with large gardens and other interesting places. We were also required to look up at night and identify constellations and planets. We were blessed to have a science teacher and others who would accompany us, give us information, and help explain some of the marvelous works of nature. I still remember those nature walks and stargazing experiences. I enjoyed them immensely!   Today,

I want to take you, my reader, on a nature walk, or indulge your attention with some relevant questions and deep thoughts. This is our first question. Where in the universe is Earth located?

According to astronomers, the universe is a vase expanse of many galaxies. A galaxy is an enormous collection of stars, up to four hundred billion of them! Earth's galaxy is called the Milky Way. Within the Milky Way, as in other galaxies, there are multiple smaller groups called solar systems. Solar systems contain planets. Earth is a planet. So cumulatively, we could say that Earth is in a solar system that is in a galaxy that is in the universe. Earth's solar system is a community of eight planets: namely, Mercury, Venus, Earth, Mars, Jupiter, Saturn Uranus, and Neptune.

Now, why do we live on Earth and not on another planet in our solar system? Which planet (s) in our solar system can support human life? To find out, let us examine some information that I gleaned from the National Aeronautics and Space Administration (NASA). I will supply some facts about each planet and at the end you will decide whether you could live there. Find at least one clue to help you decide.

Mercury

Atmosphere: The air is thin. It is comprised mostly of oxygen, sodium, hydrogen, helium, and potassium.
Temperature: It experiences extreme temperature.

Climate/**Weather**: It is blasted with solar radiation throughout.
Surface: It is solid and cratered like on Earth's moon.

Interesting fact: It is the smallest planet and the closest to the sun. It is also the fastest one with 88 days in one year.
Question: Can a human being live on Mercury?

Venus
Atmosphere: It is filled with carbon dioxide. The air pressure is comparable to the pressure that is one mile below sea-level.
Climate/Weather: It has thick, yellowish clouds of sulfuric acid that trap heat.
Temperature: It is over 900 degrees Fahrenheit. This is lead-melting heat.
Surface: It is a rusty color. It is also crowded with mountains and thousands of large volcanoes.
Interesting fact: It is the sixth largest planet and the closest to Earth. It rotates backwards. So, the sun rises in the west and sets in the east.
Question: Would you want to live on Venus?

Mars
Atmosphere: It is thin, mostly carbon dioxide, with a small amount of oxygen and water vapor.
Climate/Weather: It experiences dust storms. It looks red. It has seasons and polar caps.

Temperature: It is cold. Temperature ranges from -220 degrees to 80 degrees Fahrenheit. Average temperature is about -60 degrees. Some reports calculate it to be lower.

Surface: It is rocky with iron mineral in the dusty soil that rust. It is desert-like. It has no liquid water

Interesting fact: It is the seventh largest, in other words, the second smallest planet. The days are longer than Earth's. One-year equals to 687 Earth days.

Question: Can humans exist on Mars?

Jupiter

Atmosphere: It is hydrogen and helium, ammonia and water swirling around.

Climate/Weather: It is cold and windy with a giant storm, twice the size of Earth, churning for hundreds of years.

Temperature: It is cold.

Surface: It is a ball of gas.

Interesting fact: It is the largest planet in the solar system. It has short days and long years.

Question: Can a human being live on Jupiter?

Saturn

Atmosphere: It is comprised of hydrogen and helium

Climate/Weather: It is gassy

Temperature: It is cold.
Surface: It is a ball of hydrogen and helium.
Interesting fact: It is the second largest planet in our solar system. It has seven glorious rings of ice and rocks around it. It has short days and long years.
Question: Can human beings live on Saturn?

Uranus

Atmosphere: It is comprised of mostly molecular hydrogen, atomic helium, and methane.
Climate/Weather: It is icy and cold.
Temperature: It is cold.
Surface: It is a hot, dense fluid of water, methane, and ammonia above a small rocky core.
Interesting fact: It is the third largest planet. It rotates east to west like Venus.
Question: Can humans exist on Uranus?

Neptune
Atmosphere: It is gassy, mostly molecular hydrogen, atomic helium, and methane.
Climate/Weather: It is dark. It is cold, windy, and icy.
Temperature: It is cold and windy.
Surface: It is a ball of gas.
Interesting fact: It is the fourth largest. It has rings

of clumps of dust and debris around it. It is the only planet not visible to the naked eye. It lies the furthest from the sun.

Question: Can humans exist on Neptune?

Now here is some information about our planet home, some of which you might have been overlooking.

Earth

Atmosphere: It is comprised of hydrogen and oxygen. It also has blankets of air that protect us from heat and radiation from the sun. Other planets do not.

Climate/Weather: Earth has seasons; summer, autumn, winter, and spring. The climate varies from one place to another.

Temperature: The temperature varies. The average temperature is about 57 degrees Fahrenheit. The hottest inhabited place, Death Valley California, USA reached a record of 134 degrees Fahrenheit. The coldest inhabited place, a village in Siberia, recorded - 49 degrees Fahrenheit, as its lowest temperature. The Earth, however, gets much colder at the poles.

Surface: It has solid ground that is rocky or sandy in some places. 70% of the surface is liquid water.

Interesting fact: It is the fifth largest planet and the third away from the sun. It is the nearest to Venus whose temperature is so hot that it can melt lead. Earth is tilted on its axis, causing us to experience seasons and causing the seasons to be opposite in the Northern and Southern Hemispheres.

Question: Of all the planets in our solar system, which is the only one that sustains human life?

Earth is the only planet in our solar system on which humans live. It is also the only one that possesses the conditions that are needed to sustain human life. Now it would seem as though the earth were there, just right for human existence. However, what does the Bible say?

According to the Bible in Genesis chapters 1 and 2: 1-3, God created the earth in six days and rested on the seventh day. The Creator set the seventh day as a special one for the inhabitants of Earth to remember that he himself created it, that is Earth. Thereby, he placed his mark or royal seal on his creation. Today a week still has seven days!

Allow me to elaborate on the days for a moment. The numbering of the days since creation has been so preserved that it is traceable right back to then, even though the Romans tried to change this. The Romans called the first day of the week Sunday, in honor of the sun god that they worshipped on the first day. The second day, they called Monday, or day of the moon and so on. Since the Roman government was a world ruler, other nations and languages did likewise. Today many calendars even start the week, not with

Sunday, the first day, but with Monday, the second day.

However, all is not lost. Even though the Romans attached names of their pagan gods to the numbered days of the week, the original numbering of the days from creation remains in some languages such Portuguese, Hebrews, Arabic, Persian and modern Greek. For instance, in Portuguese, Monday is *segunda-feira,* which literally means second day. So even if they start the calendar week with Monday, they know that Monday is the second, not the first day of the week. It is simply quite interesting that traces of these numbered days remain, everything linking right back to creation!

Although God created Planet Earth and placed his seal on it, to remind us of his creative acts, some scientists report that Earth terraformed itself over billions of years. Nonetheless, the Bible says otherwise. "The Lord by wisdom founded the earth, by understanding He established the heavens. By his knowledge the depths were broken up, and clouds drop down the dew." (New King James Version Bible,1982, Proverbs 3:19).

In recent years, some pioneer-minded people have started planning to terraform another planet, meaning to form another planet to have the life sustaining conditions that exist on Earth. Stephen Hawking, an English theoretical physicist, cosmologist, and author, in a documentary titled

"Stephen Hawking Expedition New Earth" strongly suggested that humans become a multi-planetary species by colonizing another planet. The idea behind colonizing another planet was that conditions on Earth would make it too challenging for humans to continue living here.

Scientists opine that global warming could cause the melting of the ice caps, the large areas of land in the North and South Poles of the Earth that are covered with a thick layer of ice and snow. If this happens, according to National Geographic, the world could be flooded. Scientists say that the Pacific Island of Kiribati is the first island that would be covered up by the waters of rising sea levels due to climate change. The island has already lost some of its land mass to the Pacific Ocean.

Kiribati is not the only place that is experiencing rising sea levels. Parts of Miami Beach, Florida, in the United States of America, are sometimes invaded by sea water. This pattern might also exist in other countries due mostly to human activities. For example, mangroves, large shrublike plants with complex root system, grow along the shorelines in Florida. These plants help to protect the soil from erosion; however, they are often destroyed by humans.

Despite the destructive actions of humans, climate change or other challenges, the threat of a worldwide flood is nonexistent. Consider the following verses.

"I set My rainbow in the cloud,
And it shall be for the sign of the covenant
 between Me and the earth.
It shall be, when I bring a cloud over the earth,
 that the rainbow shall be seen in the cloud;
and I will remember My covenant which is between
 Me and you and every living creature of all flesh;
the waters shall never again become a flood to
destroy all flesh." (Genesis 9:12- 15).

Reading these verses, we realize that the Creator's
promise is that the entire earth will never again be
destroyed by a flood. Therefore, we do not have to
be concerned about a worldwide flood. This promise
however, does not refer to regional flooding. So,
while another flood will never destroy the earth,
areas of the earth might become flooded.
Furthermore, this promise does not exempt us from
taking care of our environment. After the Creator
formed Earth, he gave man the task of tending and
keeping it, as recorded in Genesis 2:15.

As we complete our nature walk around our solar
system, we realize that Earth is the only planet that
accommodates us. Therefore, it seems appropriate
for us to appreciate our planet home and take care of
it, without, in the process, violating the laws and
promises of our Creator.

Nugget 1:
If Earth terraformed itself over billions of years, why

hasn't any other planet in its solar system done the same? Was Earth smart enough to tilt on its axis, all by itself, to bring us the seasons? Why do you think that the Creator allowed humans to probe into space? Share your thoughts and ask questions at a live seminar.

Melinda Ferrari

24

Chapter Two

To Move or Not to Move

W ill an asteroid destroy Earth? Are you looking forward to moving to another planet? Scientist Stephen Hawkins (1942-2018) suggested that humans seek to inhabit another planet for our own good. (Kharpal,2017)

I will begin this essay by relating to you, my reader, a fascinating story about some brave people who wanted to build a safe place, way up in the sky. How high would they have to build, and did they succeed? Of course, I will also give you the other side, the more scientific side of the moving day story, afterwards. In this way, you might be better equipped to arrive at your own reasonable conclusion. I implore your patience as you read through even information you might not be keen about. It will pay off in the end

Moving Day Story One

This is not a belling of the cat story. It is a real story that happened approximately 4000 years ago. The narrative that sets the background to this story happened about 2350 B.C. −1250 B.C., over 1,500 years after Adam and Eve succumbed to Satan's evil plot, as recorded in the Bible (Genesis Chapter 3).

As the story in the Bible (Genesis Chapters. 7- 11) indicates, the population of the Earth had increased and so did evil. Consequently, the Almighty God of heaven called a man named Noah to build a ship called an ark. Since the inhabitants had become so vile, God was about to destroy the whole Earth with a flood. However, those who obeyed his laws would enter the ship and be saved. Noah built the ark and just as God had said, those who obeyed his laws entered the ark and were saved. There were only eight obedient ones, all from Noah's family.

After the flood water abated, Noah and his family emerged from the ark. Then God made them a promise. He promised them that he would never again destroy the earth with a flood. He even put his rainbow in the sky as a sign and a reminder of this promise.

Moving forward, it was on Noah's three sons and their wives the responsibility of repopulating Earth.

As they began to repopulate the world, they must have told their offspring about the great flood. So, when the generations that followed saw God's rainbow in the sky, they would be reminded of the catastrophic flood and God's wonderful promises.

Nonetheless, as the popular story goes, one generation that followed, was not taking any chances. A rainbow was not enough to assure them that God would never again destroy the earth with a flood. In other words, they had no confidence in the words of the Almighty God.

Unfortunately, their distrust resulted in a plan to defeat God, in the event of another disaster. So, they started to build a tower as the story in Genesis 11:1-19 explains. Their intention was to build a tower reaching high up to the heavens. Thus, in the event of another flood, they would climb up the tower and be saved. Thereby, that generation would have eliminated the need to depend on God or to follow his laws.

How high would this tower have to extend to save them form a flood like Noah's? The Bible, in Genesis 7:19, tells us that after the flood waters had increased, it covered the tops of the hills and mountains, and then increased 15 cubits or about 23 feet higher. If Mount Everest, the highest mountain in the world, existed in those days, at a height of 29,035 feet, I could add 23 feet to get a total of 29,058. However, the Bible also says that all the birds of the air were destroyed in Genesis 7:23. Therefore, if the Ruppel's griffon vulture, the highest-flying bird at 37,000 feet existed then, I should add 23 feet to 37,000 feet to get 37,023 feet. So, the tower would have to be more than 7 miles high to be above the flood waters or more than 13.6 times higher than the tallest building today.

Just another thought; what if God had wrapped the Earth in water, all the way up to the 62 miles of Earth's gravity! And yet another thought. The tower builders wanted to go up into the heavens. However, beyond Earth's gravity, they would have encountered the surprise of weightlessness. What would have happened then? Final thought on this: the rain fell for 40 days and nights, how many days and nights would it take these people in Shinar to walk up to the top of a tower that reached up into the heavens? Who would make it first, the flood waters or the people?

Also consider the number of days that the earth was covered with water. Noah's ark was on water for several months before it rested on Mt. Ararat which according to Google is 16, 854 feet at its highest, a little more than 3 miles. It took over 150 days later for the water to subside, so, the ark was on water for almost a year. Therefore, the Tower of Babel would be standing miles deep in water for almost a year. Would it withstand the water current? Having all this information, we know for sure that building the Tower of Babel would be no small feat.

Could these people manage to construct such a tall structure made of any material, let alone brick and asphalt, as mentioned in the Bible? We do not know if they would have achieved their goal, however, we know that nothing ordinary would have deterred them from working at it. They were not giving up. God himself said that nothing would stop them from doing what they had purposed to do. Hence, he came down and supernaturally stopped them by confounding their language. So, the project failed for lack of effective communication!

I have not found any reliable proof for the height that Babel's tower had reached when God took action to stop its construction. However, in my research, I discovered that some construction workers, builders, and architects declared that a tower made of brick and asphalt would not sustain itself for any considerable height, bearing in mind the altitude that it needed to reach. The foundations would not be able to withstand the weight of the building. Rather, the building or buildings would collapse sooner than later.

Wow! So, it would seem to me that God in his mercy came down at the right time and saved the people from their own destruction. Therefore, confounding their language, thus causing the project to cease, was a blessing!

Genesis 11: verses 3, 4 tells us that the people of Shinar wanted to stay in one location instead of being scattered over the earth. They wanted to be famous, and they wanted to build a safe place that would take them from the earth up into the heavens. That is why they decided to build the tower of Babel.

Note that God had said these words to Noah after

the flood: "Be fruitful and multiply and fill the earth." (Genesis 10:1) Therefore, the inhabitants of Earth were to fill or populate the earth, not the heavens. In addition, God promised to never destroy Earth again with a flood, and he sealed the deal with his rainbow. Whenever the rainbow appears in the sky, it reminds us of God's promise. He also promised to keep the seasons intact and cause food to grow from the ground. However, his words in Genesis 9:12-15 and 8:22 were of no importance to those people in Shinar. Rather, they interpreted them to suit their own purpose. But the Bible says the following about Gods words: "For what if some did not believe? Will their unbelief make the faithfulness of God without effect? Certainly not! Indeed, let God be true but every man a liar." (Rom. 3:3, 4).

Whatever their reason for building the tower of Babel, the people in Shinar, did not care about God's guidelines. They wanted to change God's laws for their own rules. They did not want to obey his laws as Noah did. Furthermore, they did not want to depend on God's plan to save them. They would rather be self-sufficient and save themselves. Thus, as revealed by their action, their thoughts were to escape calamity, or even the judgement of God by their own means, by creating a safe place for themselves in the heavens. In their naivety, they rejected their Creator, their only Savior.

The reasoning that led to the building of the Tower of Babel still exists in our world today even though God made the promise in this verse. "While the earth remains, Seedtime and harvest Cold and heat, Winter and summer, And day and night Shall not cease." (Gen.8:22).

In simpler terms, Earth will always experience the seasons. If Earth being tilted a certain way brings us the seasons, it will continue to be tilted that way. The sowing of seeds will continue to occur, and harvests will be reaped. Night will still turn into day as it did on the first day of creation. The sun and the moon will continue to serve us as they did from the beginning. The Creator will continue to take care of us, regardless of our situation

Moving Day Story Two

The late Stephen Hawking, who was one of the world's most prominent scientists, strongly suggested that the inhabitants of Earth establish a colony on another planet. Hawking explained his reason for suggesting that humans colonize another planet in a documentary entitled "Stephen Hawking Expedition New Earth." He explained that the danger of asteroid strikes, disease epidemic, catastrophic climate change and overpopulation would make life on Earth unbearable. Therefore, humans should **hurry** to prepare another home for themselves. That home on another planet he said would be new Earth.

However, the Bible in Isaiah 65:17 and 66:22 indicates that God himself promises to create a new earth, where distress and suffering will be non existent. 2 Peter 3:13 assures us that righteousness will dwell in the new earth. Obviously, no human would have to try to figure out how to terraform a new earth.

Hawking has found some supporters or followers who are actively seeking to terraform another planet. Will anything stop them from doing what they purpose to do. Mars, the second-smallest planet in our solar system, seems to be the candidate for terraforming since it, as reported, has a certain earthlike characteristic. Nonetheless, it should be noteworthy to mention that scientist cannot accurately calculate the distance from Earth to Mars. They approximate it to be **140 million miles or 225 million kilometers** away and getting there could take approximately 8 months using the machinery available today.

It is interesting to note that Stephen Hawking used the word *hurry* as noted above and Jesus uses the word *quickly*, referring to his return in the end-time prophetic book of Revelation. He said, "And behold, I am coming quickly, and my reward is with me, to give everyone according to his work." (Rev.22:15).

Scientist Galileo Galilei said, "The Bible shows the way to go to heaven, not the way the heavens go." Based on what we know about space today, the tower builders of Shinar certainly did not know how the heavens go, neither did they even desire to follow God's way to get to heaven. Nonetheless, they had ruthless determination. Thankfully, God's mercy prevailed.

Certainly, the inhabitants of earth will leave this planet, at least some of us. We will visit celestial places, and we will later
inhabit a new earth. Our move to somewhere else in the cosmos will happen when the prophetic time is fulfilled.

Nugget 2:

Will humans terraform another planet? Why or why not? What do you think will happen if humans move forward with their plan to terraform Mars? When will the prophetic time be fulfilled?
Find answers.

Chapter Three

Space Travel Today in the Bible

D oes the Bible mention anything about space travel? Let us explore this interrogative. Quoting President John F. Kennedy, Neil DeGrasse Tyson on StarTalk said "Space is the new frontier" which the president had said as the United States of America readied itself to embark deeper into space exploration.

In July 1969, Apollo 11 landed a man on the moon. In fact, the mission carried American Astronauts Neil Armstrong, Michael Collins, and Buzz Aldrin. As he took his first step on the surface of the moon, Armstrong remarked, "That's one small

step for man, one giant leap for mankind."
Undeniably, these words seem to have been so
divinely scripted that no other remark at any other

space expeditions can surpass them or even match
them.

Armstrong's notable remark was both a fulfilment
of Bible prophecy and a prediction of the future. I
bring your attention the following: "But you,
Daniel, shut up the words, and seal the book until the
time of the end; many shall run to and fro, and
knowledge shall increase." (Daniel 12:4).

This verse was given to Daniel, who served in the
courts of King Nebuchadnezzar of Babylon. King
Nebuchadnezzar who ruled Babylonia from about
605 to 562 BC was one of the most powerful and
ruthless kings of his time. He expanded his kingdom
by conquering many territories, one of which was
Jerusalem. Daniel was one of the smart Hebrew
young men that King Nebuchadnezzar of Babylon
took captive when he besieged Jerusalem in 597 B.C.

The Book of Daniel is one of the so-called end-
time prophetic books of the Bible. The narrative in
this book explains the sequence of events to occur
from Nebuchadnezzar's reign until the so-called end-
time.

The first indication about these end-time events
was illustrated in a dream that King Nebuchadnezzar
had but could not remember. Although he could not
remember his dream, he realized that it had some

profound significance. Considering this, he called his wise men and ordered
them, under threat of death, to tell him what he had dreamed and to interpret his dream. That was impossible for the wisemen to do. So, they requested that the king himself related the dream, and then, they could give meaning to it, but the king would have none of that. Angry at their incompetence, he decided to kill them all.

Daniel, the Hebrew wiseman, was confident that God would help him get both the dream and its interpretation for the king; therefore, he asked for more time to inquire of his God. Fortunately, Nebuchadnezzar obliged. Daniel and his friends prayed and soon, God revealed both the dream and its interpretation to Daniel.

In his dream, King Nebuchadnezzar of Babylon had seen a statue. The curious thing about this image is that it was made of different metals. The head was made of gold, the chest and arms of silver, the belly and hips of bronze, the legs of iron and the feet were made of part iron and part clay.
King Nebuchadnezzar was delighted to hear his dream and visualize the image again! However, he was not so excited about the interpretation. Each metal on the image represented a different government. The head of gold represented Babylon which was the first kingdom to rule the entire then known world. It would be overtaken by an inferior

kingdom, represented by the chest and arms of silver. King Nebuchadnezzar did not like this. His kingdom would be conquered by another.

The third world kingdom was the belly and hips of bronze and the fourth was the legs of iron. The fourth world kingdom would be the last to rule the entire world. The feet made of part iron and part clay represented the divided kingdoms or regions remaining after the fourth world kingdom was dismantled.

The king had also watched, in his dream, until a stone struck the statue on the feet, causing it to break up into pieces and convert into dust. Then the wind blew away the dust. Afterwards, the stone grew into a mountain so big that it filled the whole earth.

Now, here are the world kingdoms and we call history as our witness to help us with more specific information such as dates.

Babylonian Empire: Babylon was the head of gold and Daniel was living under this kingdom when he interpreted this dream. The Babylonian world empire ended in 539 B.C.

Medo-Persian Empire. Medo-Persia, represented by the chest and arms of silver, became the second world ruler. They ruled the world from approximately 539 to 531 B.C. Daniel himself lived to see Babylon fall to the Medes and Persians.

Secular history records that Babylon was conquered by the Medes and Persians in 539 B.C., and Biblical records show that Daniel continued to serve as wiseman under the Medo-Persian rule. So, Daniel saw a part of the prophecy fulfill.

Greek Empire: Greece represented by the belly and hips of bronze. It became the third world kingdom, ruling from 531 B.C. until 168 B.C.

Roman Empire: The Romans, represented by the legs of iron, became the fourth world rulers, and continued from 168 B.C. to A.D. 476.

Afterwards: The time after the fall of Roman rule is represented by the feet made of part iron and part clay is the time of the divided kingdoms. After the Roman Empire cascaded in A.D. 476, no other single world ruler has emerged. Napoleon Bonaparte tried, but he failed, so did Adolf Hitler. We are presently living in this divided period of iron mixed with clay.

It is during the time of the divided kingdoms, the time in which we are presently living, that the stone will smash the statue to dust and the stone will convert into a mountain and fill the earth, The stone that crushed the image at the feet and caused it to crumble represented the God of heaven who would, during the divided kingdoms, set up his kingdom that will last forever.

We have been living in the divided kingdoms since 476 A.D. In addition, almost all other prophecies that were predicted to occur between 476 A.D. and the end, have already been fulfilled, including one in 2021. When will the stone strike the image, giving way to God's everlasting kingdom? Daniel was also curious. God had also given him dreams and visions and the archangel Gabriel had given him the interpretation to them. Daniel wanted to know when all the prophecies that he had received would be realized and when the end-time would come.

The angel assured Daniel that the end of time would not come in his day, that he would pass away, rest in his grave and be resurrected to "his inheritance" in the end. This end refers to when Jesus returns. Let us now focus our attention on analyzing what the angel said. "But you, Daniel, shut up the words, and seal the book until the time of the end; many shall run to and fro, and knowledge shall increase." (Daniel 12:14).

The verse indicates that the time of the end on Earth will be marked by an increase of knowledge so sophisticated that people will have achieved the ability to travel in ways and to places that Daniel would not understand even if they were explained to him. Nonetheless, the people in the time of the end would understand. The expression *"to and fro"* spoken by the angel must include travelling up above in the firmament, in the same direction from which the angel came. This must refer to space travel, that is, humans going up into space and back. Space travel is, therefore, a sign that indicates that the inhabitants of Earth are presently living in the final portion of the end-time.

Before the angel's remark, people had been travelling from one place to another all over the surface of the then known world, long before Daniel's days. They travelled by boat, by foot, on horseback and in chariots. Certainly, King Nebuchadnezzar's army had travelled over land to the countries that they had conquered. Therefore, it would be easy for Daniel to understand if the angel had explained that travel across land would become faster and better. Therefore, *"to and fro"* must mean something else. Something that Daniel would not readily understand.

Recently, in 2021, the Virgin Galactic Unity spacecraft flight with Richard Branson went up over fifty miles into space, passing the blue sky, leaving most of Earth's atmosphere behind. During his subsequent interview on the US television program, "Today", Branson expressed his hope for the continuation of space tourism.

A few days afterwards, Jeff Bezos and his team on the Blue Virgin also launched into space. Thus began the age of space tourism. More than a decade before space tourism began, Elon Musk's Space X had created the first commercial company to fly space exploration missions, launching cargo and crew into orbit. Indeed, we are in the age of space travel! Who would have dreamed about or understood this a thousand years ago?

In summary, the Creator wants the inhabitants of Earth to know when he is about to return to redeem his creation to a better life. Therefore, he has given prophecies and released interpretations to alert us to prepare for the grand occasion. He has allowed astronauts, astrophysicists, and other scientists the knowledge that is needed to learn more about space. He has also created the ability for people to journey out into space and back. Additionally, from the tone of the text and the message in the Book of Daniel, human-conducted space travel will occur in the final portion of the end-time.

Nugget 3:

Why would the Creator of heaven and Earth want us to know when he will return? How much longer will space travel continue? Will humans use modern technology to travel to other places not yet visited in our galaxy?

Chapter Four

The Real Shape of the Earth

Greek philosopher, Aristotle (384 B.C. – 322 B.C.), noticed that stars that were visible in Egypt were not simultaneously visible in Europe. In other words, if people who lived in the Northern Hemisphere and those who lived in the Southern Hemisphere looked up at the night sky on a given date, they would not see the same stars or constellations. Aristotle used this observation as one of his convincing arguments to propose that Earth is round.   He determined that the idea of a flat Earth was impossible.

Since then, scientist have gathered even more tangible proof to substantiate Aristotle's observations. Consequently, Astrophysicist Dr. Neil DeGrasse Tyson, host of StarTalk, firmly declares that Earth is round.

Is Earth flat or is it round? There are still some conflicting thoughts on the shape of the earth. Some people think it is round while others maintain that it is flat, as many ancient cultures including early ancient Greeks, Babylonians, and Egyptians all believed. 'Flat-earthers' sometimes even use the Bible to defend their point of view. Now, what does the Bible say about the shape of Earth? First, take into consideration the following four Bible verses.

"He stretches out the north over empty space;
He hangs the earth on nothing." (Job 26:7).

"He drew a circular horizon on the face of the waters at the boundary of light and darkness." (Job 26:10).

In the beginning God created the heavens and the earth. The earth was without form, and void;
and darkness was on the face of the deep.
And the Spirit of God was hovering over the face of the waters. *(Genesis 1, 2.)*

"When he prepared the heavens,
I was there When he drew a circle on the face of the deep." (Proverbs. 8:27).

The following are four things that are made clear by the preceding texts:

1. Earth is hung in empty space. This means that

the earth does not sit on any support, and unlike a picture on a wall, it does not hang from a peg. Rather, it is there in space seemingly supported by an invisible force.

2. Earth has a circular shape. It is not a polygon by any means.

3. Earth has depth. This circular shape mentioned here in the Bible has depth; therefore, it is not flat. A flat circle has no depth.

4. Earth has a horizon with a with a boundary of light and darkness. Objects are visible in light and invisible in darkness. Therefore, a boundary of light and darkness seems to be where objects are visible one moment and the next are invisible. To illustrate this, consider the scenario of looking out at the wide-open ocean where, in the distance, the sky seems to curve to meet the waters, and ships disappear on the horizon, yet they have not fallen of the earth. Ships can also appear on the horizon. This boundary of light and darkness is also evident in the morning when the sun is visible, portion by portion, as it slowly rises over the eastern horizon, dismissing the darkness of the night, moment by moment. This occurs again, in the

evening, as the sun sinks into the western sky, causing darkness to reappear.

If the sun were shining over a flat earth, it would need to be switched out, causing all its light to disappear at once and the deep blackness of night to appear instantly. (So much thought went into creating Earth!)

It might be important to note here that Bible writers were inspired by the Holy Spirit, many through visions, and sometimes, they saw objects with which they were not acquainted. Subsequently, they lacked the vocabulary to name them. Therefore, in lieu of naming, they described what they saw. "He drew a circular horizon on the face of the waters at the boundary of light and darkness" above is a descriptive sentence.

Now before further analyzing the information that has been gathered so far, look at two verses where the Bible mentions "the ends of the earth" and "the four corners of the earth."

"After these things I saw four angels standing
at the four corners of the earth,
 holding the four winds of the earth,
 that the wind should not blow on the earth,
 on the sea, or on any tree." (Acts 1:8).

"But you shall receive power
when the Holy Spirit comes on you:
and you will be my witnesses in Jerusalem,

and in Judea and Samaria and to the ends of the earth." (Revelation 7:1).

When the Bible mentions "the ends of the earth" and "the four corners of the earth" it simply means everywhere in the east, west, north, and south. These are idiomatic expressions. Therefore, a message that is going out to "the ends of the earth" or to "the four corners of the earth" goes to every part of the earth. It is intended to reach all the inhabitants of the earth and has no application to the shape of Earth.

Now consider the properties of some familiar shapes. Is the biblical explanation of the shape of the earth more like a polygon, circle, or sphere? A polygon is not circular, and it has no depth. Let us eliminate that one. A circle has no depth, and so it does not allow for the boundary of light and darkness where things seem to disappear while they are still on the circle.

One more observation that sheds additional light on the shape of Earth is this verse. "The wind goes toward the south And turns around to the north; The wind whirls about continually And comes again on its circuit." (Ecclesiastes. 1:6). This verse paints a picture of the wind completing a circular journey by moving around the earth, starting at the north, going south and back to the north. This must be a spherical object.

The biblical explanation of Earth is a circular shape that has depth and a boundary of light and darkness. This description more closely fits a sphere than any other known shape. In addition, scientists have taken videos from space that reveal a rotating spherical Earth. Hence, it is reasonable to conclude that the earth is not flat, but round.

Undoubtedly, the Bible records that the earth is round, and now astronomy confirms it, and the world can witness it. Was this discovery a deliberate plan of a supreme being?

Nugget 4:

It is quite interesting that whatever is visible in the Northern Hemisphere is not simultaneously visible in the Southern Hemisphere. It is interesting to me because Jesus explains that when he returns, every inhabitant on Earth will look up and see him above, in the air, all at once. (Revelation 1:7) This must be a supernatural event that will make the second coming of the Messiah, Jesus, inimitable. Only the Creator can cause such astronomical phenomenon to happen! How might this happen.

Chapter Five

The Age of the Earth

How old is Planet Earth, billions of years, or thousands of years? In general, there are two fields of thoughts on the age of the earth. There are the scientists who claim that Earth is approximately 4.5 billion years old. On the other hand, there are the opponents, called creationists, who assert that the earth is approximately six thousand years old.

How could two groups arrive at such differing numbers for the age of the earth? Before taking sides or ridiculing either group, it should prove helpful to examine some relevant details that I have researched from both fields of thoughts that have helped me arrive at my conclusion.

First, let us examine the scientists' method of calculation. According to my research, scientists mainly analyze the constituents of the oldest rocks and the movements of the earth in their quest to arrive at the age of the earth.

According to geologists, the crust of the Earth itself changes annually, resulting in different stages of its formation, in the same way that a tree acquires a distinctive ring that marks each year of its existence. Hence, the key to determining the evolution of the earth lies in comparing the present crust to the depleted ones. So, rock samples gathered from the earth's crust are employed as geologic timekeepers.

In addition, scientists observe the rate at which geologic changes occur in the earth, impacted by processes such as erosions, volcanic actions, caters and tectonics. In the process, they have dated locations such as the Hawaiian Islands, the Atlantic Ocean, the East Coast of South America, and the West Coast of Africa. They have even studied the movements of the continents.

Furthermore, scientists have also used radiometric dating, to measure the distinctive properties of radioactive materials in the earth. They measure elements such as carbon and uranium in rocks, water, and air, which according to scientists, break apart and decay in a timely manner, like the predictable ticks of a clock.

Scientists have even looked to space for help by

using the oldest known meteorites formed within the solar system to arrive at the age of the Earth. Having done such extensive work to arrive at their calculation, scientists are satisfied that their estimate for the age of the earth is correct. How then can anyone think otherwise?

Creationists use the Bible to determine the age of the earth. Might they have a valid claim? Their calculation begins at creation week; hence, they are called creationists. One of the most prominent was James Ussher (1581 - 1656) an archbishop whose writings were published in 1650.

Ussher calculated the number of years from Adam to the birth of Christ and from the birth of Christ to 1652. Adam was created in the first year of creation, on the sixth day of creation week. Ussher followed the genealogy in the Bible via the ages of the patriarchs from Adam to Jacob which are clearly recorded in the Bible. He continued his calculation factoring in the other periods such as the years that the Israelites spent in slavery, the passage through the wilderness, the reign of the judges and kings of Israel and the Babylonian captivity. He also cross-referenced secular records such the reigns of the world kingdoms and the calendars of the day. Based on his calculations, Ussher proposed that creation week started in 4004 BC. The added 4 might be to compensate for some miscalculations of the Julian calendar, regarding the birth of Jesus.

When we adjust Ussher's calculations to 2021, the age of the Earth would be about 6000 years.

There are literally billions of years difference between 6000 and 4.4 billion. Stay alert for the clincher that lies ahead as we go searching for the difference.

Is there any information in the Bible that might support the scientists or may offer more depth to the creationists' argument? "In the beginning God created the heaven and the earth. And the earth was without form, and void; and darkness was upon the face of the deep. And the Spirit of God moved upon the face of the waters" (Genesis 1:1, 2).

Here the Bible records that when God started to create the earth, there was something that already existed. What already existed was darkness and water, and the water was deep! Now God, the Master Artist, was ready to form Earth to make it suitable to sustain life as we know it.

The water had been standing there before God decided to form it into Planet Earth and populate it. How much time had passed since the darkness and water, with its contents, were created and left there? Was it six thousand, six million or even six billion years?

On the second day of creation, God caused the waters to divide, creating a space with water above and below as recorded in Genesis 1:6-8. There was water below, space between and water above. Now, notice what happens on the third day of creation.

"And God said, Let the waters under the heaven be gathered together unto one place, and let the dry

land appear and it was so.
And God called the dry land Earth;
and the gathering together of the waters called he
Seas: and God saw that it was good." (Genesis 1:9,
10)

So, the water shifted, and dry land came up.
Notice that the Bible specifically stated, "let the dry
land appear", not just land. God wanted the land to
be dry, not wet. So, the ground came up out of the
waters, above sea level, and it was dry. Was there
wet land under the waters before he called it to come
up dry?

One of the meanings of appear is *to* come into
sight or to become visible. This meaning is similar
in other languages, too. The Hebrew root of the verb
that means to appear, as used in the Bible, reflects a
similar meaning. Additionally, it might be helpful
to note some synonyms of the word appear such *as*
to come into view, to expose and *to come out*. The
following verse may shed more light on the subject.

You who laid the foundations of the earth,
So that it should not be moved forever,
You covered it with the deep as with a garment;
The waters stood above the mountains.
At Your rebuke they fled;
At the voice of Your thunder they hastened away.
They went up over the mountains;
They went down into the valleys,
To the place which You founded for them.
You have set a boundary that they may not pass

over
That they may not return to cover the earth. (Psalm
104:5 -7)

Analyzing the verse, we see that it was God himself who had laid or made the foundation of the earth, that is, the ground, and the water, from which Planet Earth was formed. When God commanded "and let the dry land appear" the waters moved away from the valleys and over mountains (obviously underwater valleys and mountains) to gather in one place as seas.

One might argue that the ground was not there before, it only came up via the water. However, if the dry land had come up out of the water, then the dry land might certainly contain some of the properties of the water that had been standing there for some time. Consequently, some of the constituents of the water might be traceable in the dry land, making Earth's crust reveal characteristics as old as the water from which it came up. Thus, the length of time that the water was there would be what really counts in determining the age of the dry ground.

Who knows how long the foundation of the earth had been already formed by the Creator before he made it habitable for the first couple, Adam and Eve, whom he created, along with other life forms! Even though the Bible does not disclose the age of the crust of the earth, it offers valuable insights about its existence before creation week. That time of existence could be billions of years! This could mean that the calculation of scientists incorporates a time earlier than creation week if their calculation is accurate.

Creationists, however, begin their calculations at the first day of the 7-day creation week as stated in Genesis Chapter 1:1-31 and 2: 1-3, in which God created the following:

Day 1: Light
Day 2: The firmament
Day 3: Land and vegetation
Day 4: The great lights: Sun, moon, and stars
Day 5: Birds, marine life, and creeping things
Day 6: Land animals and human beings
Day 7: The Sabbath. On day seven, God rested and set apart the seventh day as a seal or memorial of his marvelous work.

Indeed, the Bible provides ample information to facilitate the calculation of the length of time since creation week to be approximately 6000 years to date!

Both scientists and creationists have provided evidence to prove their point. However, they seem to be working with two different starting points. Creationists began at creation week and calculated from that time forward to present time, but scientists began at present time and calculated backwards to earlier times.

Nugget 5:

Something was already there at the beginning of creation week when God started to make Earth suitable for human existence. Learn more. It might also be interesting to know that the angels had already been created, including Lucifer who had already sinned and turned Satan. Earth does not seem to be where life started in the universe.

Chapter Six

Escaping Earth's Gravity?

W hat holds the inhabitants of Earth in place? Earth is a spherical object; therefore, the inhabitants of Earth reside all over the surface of this sphere, yet no one has ever fallen off into space.

According to astrophysicists, gravity, also called gravitation is that controlling force that keeps us grounded on Earth. In other words, gravity is the pull that keeps objects together in space and keep them in place. For example, it keeps the planets in orbit around the sun, and it keeps people in place on Earth. Gravity also pulls light towards Earth.

Isaac Newton, in the 17th century, after watching an apple fall straight down, not sideways, or upwards, realized that there exists a force that keeps earthlings in place. Hence, Isaac Newton, mathematician, physicist, astronomer, and author, is credited with discovering gravity. Today, Newton's name and his mathematical formula are recognized around the world.

Astrophysicist Neil deGrasse Tyson, on StarTalk explains that Earth's gravity extends to approximately 62 miles or 100 kilometers away from the surface of the earth. At this height Earth's atmosphere begins to diminish as it blends into the gravity above. Imagine Earth as a ball, its surface being enveloped in sixty-two miles of air of a certain quantity and quality. This air does not exist at a certain height above the earth, neither does it exist in the ocean. Gravity must be vital to our existence.

The earth, other planets, and objects in space, are all held there, in place, unattached to anything visible. They are kept in place by one of the invisible things that God created, and that is gravity. Indeed, the Bible recorded the following verse thousands of years ago! "He stretches out the north over empty space; He hangs the earth on nothing." (Job 26:7).

Amazingly, less dense gravity in outer space keeps planets in orbit, and astronauts floating around with little control of their movements. Imagine that the gravity on the earth were like that on the space station! We would all be bumping into one another all day long. We would encounter dire mobility challenges daily, trying to maintain our balance. Fortunately, gravity keeps us grounded on

Earth, and thereby productive. As a bonus, it also provides for us the air that we breathe, with just the right amount of oxygen and more. The Creator must have invested some thoughts in supplying Earth with just enough gravity. How wonderful!

Will humans ever escape Earth's gravity? Humans have been planning to defy gravity long before the Wright brothers built the first airplane. We wanted to fly like a bird and soar like a kite. So today, we have several space vehicles that travel within Earth's gravity and in outer space. Nonetheless, man cannot exist in outer space. He must return within the boundaries of Earth's confining gravity.

The writer of the article, "Return to Earth: An Astronauts view of Coming Home" explains that astronauts experience dizziness, weightlessness and, at times, nausea in space. Their body works hard to compensate as fluid rises to the torso. It takes about a week for them to begin working in weightlessness. (Chiao, 2016). Leo Chiao is a reputable source of this information since he himself was a National Aeronautics and Space Administration (NASA) astronaut who flew four missions into space and performed six spacewalks.

There have been biblical references of people who have defied Earth's gravity and presently live elsewhere beyond the sky. One such person is Elijah the prophet of God who when up into heaven in a chariot of fire. He was later seen by Peter, James and John, disciples of Jesus' inner circle, when he returned to visit Jesus, approximately two hundred years after he (Elijah) had ascended in the chariot of fire.

Another person who defied Earth's gravity was Jesus, at his ascension, he went up into heaven on a cloud while his disciples watched the entire event. The Bible says,

"Now when He had spoken these things,
while they watched, He was taken up,
and a cloud received Him out of their sight.
And while they looked steadfastly toward heaven as
He went up, behold, two men stood by them in
white apparel, who also said, Men of Galilee,
why do you stand gazing up into heaven?
This same Jesus, who was taken up from you into
heaven, will so come in like manner as you saw
Him go into heaven." (Acts 1:9-11)

Did Jesus part Earth's gravity as Moses parted the Red Sea? Before I continue with Jesus' ascension, let me briefly remind you who Moses was and how the parting of the Red Sea happened.

Moses was a Hebrew born at a time when the Israelites were slaves in Egypt, and the pharaoh had commanded that all Hebrew male babies be cast into the river Nile. Pharoah's daughter who was childless found Moses by the river and adopted him. Unbeknown to her, she employed Moses' own mother to be his baby-sitter. Therefore, Moses was brought up with both the privilege of royalty and a

Hebrew education. Later, when Moses, all grown up, murdered an Egyptian while defending a Hebrew slave. Then he became a fugitive and fled to the wilderness where he got married to a Midianite and started a new life.

While Moses was living in the Midian, God appeared to him in a burning bush and commissioned him to deliver the Hebrews (Israelites), descendants of Abraham, from slavery. Consequently, Moses returned to Egypt. There, God sent ten plagues upon Egypt. Eventually, God's people were released from slavery.

However, not long after they escaped, the Egyptians had a change of heart and perused them with the intent to recapture them. As the narrative unfolded, Moses and his people came upon the Red Sea that obstructed their path while the Egyptian army behind pursued them. Then God instructed Moses to stretch his rod across the Red Sea. Moses obeyed and immediately, a path was made through the Red Sea. The gravity over the surface of the earth had to have descended into the deep path created by the rolling back of the waters of the Red Sea for the Israelites to safely walk through to the other side.

Now back to Jesus' ascension. If Jesus parted gravity, did gravity from outer space fill the parted space causing him to float up into the heaven. Well, we do not know, and the rest of his journey back to heaven is beyond all human reckoning. The Bible, in 1 Thessalonians 4:16, Philippians 3:21 and

Revelation 20: 4, also portrays a picture of a vast number of people, with new bodies, going up into the air, up to a place in heaven to spend a thousand years with Jesus.

Therefore, it seems logical to conclude that for humans to escape Earth's gravity and live a successful life elsewhere in the universe, that place must be earthlike. It must possess the qualities of Earth that make it suitable for human life. Otherwise, human beings would have to be transformed into a new body that can reside in that place.

Nugget 6:

It appears Earth's gravitation was set in place when the firmament was created, even though it took us thousands of years to discover gravity. Is it by mere chance that humanity has discovered gravity? Is it possible for humans to develop the ability to adapt to the gravity in outer space?

Chapter Seven

Why is the Universe Expanding?

hy would the universe be expanding? The expanding universe is an amazing discovery! In the 1920's American astronomer Edwin Hubble and others discovered that most galaxies are receding from the Milky Way. They then concluded that the universe was expanding.

What I understand from this discovery is that there now lies more space between Earth's galaxy and the rest of the galaxies, and that space is becoming increasingly larger. Now this question comes to mind. Why are we being separated from the rest of whatever exists? To be separated from a group sometimes means to be on time-out for some infraction that you committed and for which you will be punished shortly. For what will the inhabitants of the earth be punishment and when will punishment be administered?

Today, I choose to take a brighter route. How about the universe expanding for a happier reason? This happier reason was mentioned by Jesus over 2000 years ago, and by mentioning it, he implied that the universe would indeed be expanding. However, before I expound on what Jesus said, it might be necessary for me to briefly explain who he is, and to present the context within which his *universe expanding* implication was expressed.

According to the Bible, Jesus was the Messiah, sent to Earth by God, the Creator of the universe. Jesus had come to Earth in human flesh to redeem mankind from sin. About 4000 years before he came, the first couple, Adam and Eve had disobeyed God by eating fruit from the tree of the knowledge of good and evil, from which God had forbidden them to eat.

Now the punishment for disobeying God's law was death; that is, total eradication from the universe. However, God, in his loving kindness and mercy already, had a plan. The plan was that the Messiah would come in human flesh and die in the couple's behalf. Subsequently, all the descendants of Adam and Eve would be eligible for redemption and salvation. Those who accepted this gift of mercy and obeyed God's laws would receive salvation. They would bypass the punishment of eternal death.

About 4 B.C Jesus was born of a virgin. He grew up and started his ministry. Many people might have heard about Jesus and his twelve close followers whom we call his disciples. After Jesus had fulfilled his part of the salvation agreement and was about to return to heaven, he made this universe expanding implication. This is what he said to his disciples:

"Let not your heart be troubled;
you believe in God, believe also in Me.
In My Father's house are many mansions;
if it were not so, I would have told you.
I go to prepare a place for you.
And if I go and prepare a place for you,
I will come again and receive you to Myself;
that where I am, there you may be also." (John 14:1-3)

So, in this verse, Jesus promised a second return to Earth, but this second coming would only be to get his people off the planet and to another location, a mansion. A mansion is a huge house. However, when Jesus mentioned *mansions,* was he referring to galaxies, planets, or literal huge houses? Certainly, the disciples knew nothing about space, galaxies, or planets; therefore, Jesus would not have used that vocabulary. These terminologies were reserved for our time. One thing is sure, and that is, to house many people, expansion is necessary.

How many people would Jesus be preparing to

house and for how long? Now let us take some logistics into account. Jesus would not only be preparing a place for his disciples who were present at his return trip to heaven. His provision would extend to include believers since the time that sin entered the world up to the time of his second coming. These include both his living and the dead followers.

The book of the Revelation of Jesus Christ describes the people Jesus will picked up on his second coming thus: "Blessed are those who do His commandments, that they may have the right to the tree of life and may enter through the gates into the city." (Revelation 22:14). Jesus himself, while he was on Earth with his twelve disciples, said, "If you love me keep my commandments." (John 14:15. The book of Revelation reveals that there will be a resurrection of all the righteous dead since the beginning of the earth and Thessalonians confirms it.

"For the Lord himself shall descend from heaven with a shout,
with the voice of the archangel, and with the trump of God:
and the dead in Christ shall rise first:
Then we which are alive and remain
shall be caught up together with them in the clouds, to meet the Lord in the air:
and so shall we ever be with the Lord. (1 Thessalonians 4: 16 – 17)

The main idea of this text is that by the time Jesus

returns, he will have prepared a place for all the righteous dead since the beginning of the world and all the righteous living at his return. That sounds like a vast number to me. In fact, Revelation 7: 9, speaking about the people who are saved when Jesus comes says, "After these things I looked, and behold, a great multitude which no one could number of all nations, tribes, peoples, and tongues, standing before the throne and before the Lamb, clothed with white robes, with palm branches in their hands."

Here we have a number so large that no human can count. Therefore, it is not millions neither is it billions, nor trillions; it is numberless. That simply means many of us, human beings, will be going up into outer space, up into the heavens for a vacation. The Bible states, "And they lived and reigned with Christ for a thousand years." (Revelation 20: 4).

This vacation time will not be for only one day. On the contrary, it will be for a literal one thousand years; therefore, it must involve some detailed planning. Since Jesus would be creating places, one assumes that the universe would be experiencing some degree of expansion. Additionally, the Bible mentions a colossal city that will come down out of heaven to be situated on the new earth. We have no details about the size of the new earth and where exactly it will be built. However, we have detailed information about the dimensions of its capital city, New Jerusalem.

We also know the size of the city. New Jerusalem, measures twelve thousand furlongs, that is approximately 1,500.3 square miles. Its length, width, and height are equal in measurement. Therefore, it seems to be a cube (Revelation 21:16). The wall of Jerusalem is 144 cubits or 72 yards high. Multiply that by 3 and it equals 216 inches. The wall has twelve foundations which are decorated with twelve different kinds of stones: namely, jasper, sapphire, chalcedony, emerald, sardonyx, sardius, chrysolite, beryl, topaz, chrysoprase, jacinth, and amethyst. The city has twelve gates, each decorated with a different kind of pearl. Note that Revelation also states that angels stand at the gates.

True to his word, the Messiah must be presently creating space for his followers. He showed up on time for the first advent; therefore, he will make the necessary preparations and return on time to gather his saints. Besides, the Creator of Earth is always creating; thus, the universe must be expanding!

Nugget 7:

The discovery that the universe is expanding could serve to motivate the inhabitants of Earth to be prepared for the grand occasion of Jesus' second coming. If he kept his promise for the first advent, would he not keep it for the second one? What do you think? Learn more.

Indeed, we must be thankful for the inquisitive scientific minds that the Creator enabled to make this wonderful observation in the heavens above.

Chapter Eight

Questions and Answers about Extraterrestrials

This essay will answer some of the profoundest questions about extraterrestrial such as whether they really exist, what they look like and their impact upon our world. It will also reveal whether you could become an extraterrestrial.

An extraterrestrial is often described as an intelligent being that inhabits somewhere outside planet Earth. Extraterrestrials or aliens are described as humanoid creatures who reside somewhere in space and visit Earth from time to time. These extraterrestrials have often been linked to flying saucers or unidentified flying objects (UFOs), and more recently rephrased unidentified aerial phenomena (UAP).

Over the years, people have reported witnessing the landing of a UFO, seeing aliens or having been abducted by them. Alien sightings came to the forefront in 1947 with the famous sighting of a flying saucer near Roswell, New Mexico, in the United States of America. The Roswell Daily Record reports that a flying saucer was captured in the region. To date, there have been thousands of reports of UFO sightings in several states in the USA; most of them in California, Florida, Washington, Texas, New York, and Arizona.

The government of the United States of America investigated about 144 sightings of UAPs and returned to the public with an interesting report. They reported that the sightings were either airborne clutter, birds, weather balloons, natural atmospheric phenomena or other. The report was both encouraging and disappointing. People who do not believe in aliens were elated, while the believers lost their thrill or almost did. Hollywood continues to treat the imagination with fascinating alien movies. However, more recent sightings of high velocity UAPs have become a cause of concern to the government.

Neil deGrasse Tyson, an American astrophysicist, planetary scientist, author, science communicator and director of the Hayden Planetarium, opines that it is unlikely that the inhabitants of Earth are the only intelligent beings in this vast universe. Nonetheless he is skeptical about certain reported sightings as he needs tangible proof.

Kindly allow me to note that Earth dwellers are not the only residents in the universe. Long before modern space exploration began, Earth was visited by extraterrestrials. Even today, it is presently being visited by extraterrestrials and it will continue to be visited by them in the future. The following are some questions and answers about extraterrestrials or aliens.

Question 1: If extraterrestrials exist, why don't scientists and others see them?

Answer: The fact that human beings lack the capacity to see an object does not make the object non-existent. We can use microorganisms that lives on Earth as an example. They exist but we do not see them. Microorganisms are too tiny to be seen by the naked eye; therefore, we use a microscope to see them. In a similar way, extraterrestrials, operating in another dimension, might not be visible to our naked eye. Furthermore, our most powerful telescopes might not be able to detect them. Also, what if they could make themselves visible or invisible. Then they could choose to be either, at their convenience.

Question 2: What do extraterrestrials look like?

Answer: Extraterrestrials are not funny creatures who get to Earth by landing on spaceships. The ones that have made themselves visible look like humans, with some having extra features. They have feet, hands, and even a mouth with which they ate the food that the humans they visited offered them. There are recorded examples to testify of these occurrences.

Question 3: Do extraterrestrials travel by spacecraft?
Answer: They do not need a spacecraft to travel across the cosmos. Space is their terrain. Many of them are known to regularly travel through space to Earth to attend to the needs of humans. Humans do not yet know how to manipulate the forces of nature to travel in space without the use of a mechanical device; perhaps that is why we equate alien travel with a device such as a spacecraft.

Question 4: Why are extraterrestrials mysterious?
Answer: Anything that lives beyond our sky or is believed to live above Earth's atmosphere, is mysterious to us. For thousands of years, above us only existed the sun, moon, and stars and beyond the sky, the unseen heavens where God resides. Humans could not perceive anything else beyond the sky. The sky was the maximum distance visible to humans. What lay beyond it was mysterious.

In recent times, the invention of telescopes has equipped us to see beyond the sky. Now we can see vast arrays of galaxies beaming throughout the universe. Consequently, we now realize that Earth occupies only a minuscular part of the universe. Now we wonder who or what else exists out there. So, extraterrestrial have always been mysterious to humans and continue to be so.

Question 5: Are there really aliens out there in space? Are there living beings on other planets?

Answer: My research has revealed that extraterrestrials do inhabit the universe and I have grouped them into four categories.

Four Categories of Extraterrestrials

These four categories are as follows:

A. Extraterrestrials who live elsewhere in the universe but **do** visit Earth.

B. People who once walked the Earth, but were taken, and now occupy some space above.

C. Extraterrestrials who live on other planets and do not visit Earth.

D. Extraterrestrials who are illegal occupants on Earth

I will now clarify this information:

A. Extraterrestrials who live elsewhere in the Universe but do visit Earth

Many people know about angels. Most of us know the nativity song "Angels we Have Heard on High." People sing it at least once a year. Angels do not live on Earth even though they do work here, or at least some of them.

The Bible clearly explains that angels do exist, and it also mentions three categories of angels. Genesis 3:24 mentions cherubim; Isaiah 6: 2-6, Seraphim and 1 Thessalonians 4:16 and Jude 1:19, the archangel.

These are intelligent beings who were made before human beings were created. They were created a little higher than human beings (Psalm 8:5), and they are equipped with multiple wings that enable them to fly through space. No spacecraft is necessary.

Another remarkable thing about angels is that they are invisible to the human eye; however, they can make themselves visible to us. Colossians 1:16 stated that God created both the visible and invisible. Hebrews 13:2 reminds us to be hospitable to strangers per adventure the strangers turn out to be angels.

Multiple verses in the Bible, including Matthew 18:10, Genesis 28:12 and Luke 23:43, indicate that the angels of God live in heaven. They are messengers from heaven whose charge is to attend to the inhabitants of Earth as the Creator indicates. Indeed, Hebrews 1:14 describes angels as spirits who God sends to minister to human beings!

An example of heavenly angels taking care of a human being is recorded in 1 Kings chapter 19. Elijah, God's prophet, received a death threat from Jezebel, the queen. Then he became so scared that he ran away. He was depressed, tired and hungry when he finally sat down under a tree and prayed that he would just die. He fell asleep. It was then that an angel touched him and told him to get up and eat. He awoke and found a cake baked on coals and a jar of water laying by his head. Elijah ate the cake and drank the water, and then, he went right back to sleep. The angel woke him up a second time and he ate the cake and drank the water that the angel had provided.

We find another example in Genesis 18. Angels appeared to Abraham, and they sat down with him and had an intelligent conversation. In fact, they talked as they ate the food that he had provided!

There is a wealth of information about angels, not only from the Bible but in current time. From time-to-time, people report being visited and assisted by angels when they find themselves helpless in difficult situations. God's angels are extraterrestrials who work on Earth to protect us help us reconnect with the Creator of the universe.

B. People who once walked the Earth, but were taken, and now occupy some space above.

The Bible, in Genesis 4: 24 and Hebrews 11: 5, testify to the fact that Enoch, son of Jared who was born in 622 A.M (Anno Mundi) was taken by God alive up into heaven at age 365. Therefore, he must have been taken about 987 A.M. My calculations show that to be approximately 3017 B.C, over 5000 years ago.

The second person in chronological order who was taken to heaven was called Moses. This is the same Moses who led the children of Israel out of Egypt's bondage about 1440 B.C. Forty years after Moses had led the Israelites from Egypt through the desert, he died on Mount Horeb where angels attended him. God did not allow him to enter the

Melinda Ferrari

Promised Land. Jude 1:9 indicates that Moses was resurrected by Michael the archangel and taken to heaven.

The third person was called Elijah. 2 Kings chapter 2 relates the ascension of Elijah who was taken up alive to heaven in a chariot of fire and horses of fire in a whirlwind. Elijah was a prophet in the northern kingdom of Israel during the reign of King Ahab. Calculating the reigns of the kings, Ahab ruled about 874-853 BC. Hence Elijah might have been taken within those years.

All three men have spent more time residing in another place in the universe other than Earth. Hence, they could be classified as extraterrestrials. There have been no report or sighting of Enoch since; however, Moses and Elijah reportedly visited Earth in approximately A.D 27. While Jesus was on the mount with Peter, James, and John, the trio witnessed Moses and Elijah appear to Jesus (Matthew 17: 1 - 3). They saw the visitors talk with Jesus. The disciples did not report hearing what Moses, Elijah and Jesus talked about; nevertheless, it is understood that Moses had come, symbolic of the righteous dead and Elijah, the righteous living, who would be saved only if Jesus accomplished his mission. Therefore, they might have been there to support and encourage him.

Before we move on, allow me to clarify something important. When a person dies, he or she does not wander around the earth in the form of a spirit. Your dead relative cannot come back to help you. He or she is not an extraterrestrial. The Bible says, "For the living know that they will die; But the dead know nothing, they have no more reward, For the memory of them is forgotten." (Ecclesiastes 9:5). Rewards here means they have not pleasure in anything. They are dead.

In several instances, the Bible refers to the dead as being in their graves until the judgment. Jesus himself, speaking of the dead says this: "Do not marvel at this; for the hour is coming in which all who are in the graves will hear His voice and come forth—those who have done good, to the resurrection of life, and those who have done evil, to the resurrection of condemnation." (John 5:28-29)

A sampling of the resurrection of the righteous happened at Jesus' crucifixion and resurrection. (Matthew 27: 50 -53.) This also proves that when people die, they do not go to heaven, but sleep in their graves until the resurrection at the end of time.

C Extraterrestrials who live on other planets and do not visit Earth.

There are intelligent beings who inhabit other planets. However, there is little information about those extraterrestrials who live on other planets because they do not visit Earth or might never have visited Earth. So, how does one arrive at the conclusion that intelligent beings inhabit other planets? Upon reading the first chapter in the Book of Job, the reader finds Satan in the presence of God at an unnamed location in the universe. He showed up.

To set the scene, let me divert a minute and remind you who Satan is. He was once Lucifer, a powerful holy angel of God, who wanted to be like God. Pride and envy had entered his life. Following this he caused other angels to distrust God; consequently, God cast him out of heaven. Satan then migrated to Earth where he tempted the newly created couple, Adam and Eve, and caused them to disobey God. After the couple disobeyed God, Satan assumed the leadership that was Adam's.

Now back to the meeting place where Satan showed up. Job 1:6 explains that the sons of God had gathered, assumedly for a meeting, when Satan appeared along with them. God asked Satan where he had come from, and he indicated Earth, in no uncertain fashion. He said, "From going to and fro on the earth, and from walking back and forth on it." He was showing some authority, some right to walking around on Earth. Satan seemed to have been bragging about his cunning ability to create havoc on Earth and usurp the leadership position.

Satan had claimed Earth, but God assured him that he (God) had people there who were still faithful to him. Here one deduces that the gathering of the sons of God might have been a meeting of the heads of the inhabitants of different worlds or planets.

This narrative suggests that there are other intelligent beings living on other planets in the universe. The way in which Satan was interrogated suggests that God was asking "Who do you think you are representing and what are you doing here? You have no business here." The situation also seems to suggest that the inhabitants of the other planets or locations in the universe were God-obeying beings, not sinners like us.

D. Extraterrestrials who are illegal occupants on Earth

As was previously mentioned, Lucifer was a resident in heaven where God abides. He was an angel of high ranking, who later rebelled against God. He also caused one-third of the holy angels to fall. God cast Lucifer out of heaven into space. Lucifer's name became Satan. Satan eventually took up residence on Earth, after he caused Adam and Eve to disobey God. It was then that Satan assumed the position of manager of Earth.

Jude 1:6 affirms that the proper domain or place of Lucifer and the fallen angels is in heaven, but they abandoned it. So, they are condemned. They were supposed to be in heaven, not on Earth. Notwithstanding, Satan and his fallen angels have taken up residency on Earth.

Although Satan and the fallen angels cannot return to their holy duties, they presently still possess their ability to travel in space and to work wonders. 2 Corinthian 11: 14 explains that Satan will pretend to be a righteous angel to convince humans to believe his deceptive plots. No wonder Jesus warns his disciples to be careful of impersonators, especially in the end time.

Jesus' sacrifice on the cross provided salvation for all mankind and made him (Jesus) the rightful Ruler on Earth. He is also the called the second Adam, since he redeemed what Adam had lost to Satan and his evil angels.

Considering the information herein, we must conclude that Satan and his fallen angels are extraterrestrials who are illegal occupants on Earth. They are dangerous beings who work to destroy the inhabitants of Earth. It might be interesting to note that Revelation chapter 20 explains that, after Jesus' second coming, Satan and his evil angels will be bound on Earth for a thousand years. They will not be able to travel outside of Earth. That seems to indicate that Satan and his evil angels can presently fly through space outside of Earth's atmosphere!

Question 6: When will the city, with aliens, hover over Earth, and how big will this space object be?
Answer: The city, New Jerusalem, 375 mile long by 375 miles wide, will hover over Earth in approximately 1000 years in the future.

Question 7: Could you become an extraterrestrial?
Answer: As mentioned above, there were three human beings who became extraterrestrials, two of them even returning to Earth for a short visit. You and I can also become extraterrestrials because Jesus promised that he would return and take his followers back to heaven. He said, "And if I go and prepare a place for you, I will come again and receive you to

Myself, that where I am, there you may be also."
(John 14:3), and we also have written report from
those who saw him go up into the heavens.
Revelation 20:4-6 explains that the saints will spend
1000 year in heaven before returning to hover over
Earth on the city called the New Jerusalem. Anyone
who meets the criteria can become a part of this
group of extraterrestrials.

In conclusion, we know that earthlings are not the
only intelligent beings in the universe. We have
company, and not all of them are righteous. The
good ones are our friends, so they seek to help us,
while the malicious ones hate us and cause havoc on
Earth as they seek to destroy us.

Nugget 8:

When Satan was cast out of heaven, did he have to
come to Earth? Could he have gone to another planet
or location in the universe? I wonder.

Chapter Nine

Amazing Benefits of Space Exploration

A mazing space videos! Have you ever watched a live view of the moon's surface? Or maybe you have watched Earth from space, viewed from the International Space Station (ISS). Looking up into space seems to have become an obsession nowadays, and videos of space have become increasingly popular and accessible. A live space tour is available to everyone from all corners of the earth, using the ubiquitous smartphone.

By the way, whose idea was it to look up at the sky and take notes? Certainly, that was what started our preoccupation with looking up. People of all cultures and civilizations throughout history have looked up at the sky and have taken notes. These include the ancient Mayans, Babylonians, and Egyptians, who left behind tangible proof of their work. To me looking up and observing is the first phase of space exploration. What these ancient peoples observed with the naked eye were only the moon and stars by night and the sun by day. However, all of this set us on the amazing journey into space today.

The second phase of space exploration, for me, would be to investigate space not only with the naked eye but to be aided by the lenses of the telescope. The third phase would be to send probes into space and the fourth to send humans into space.

The following are a few of the myriads of ways in which space has impacted our lives.

Wellness. The sun and moon, not only give light, but they help to keep us healthy many other ways. They help us to do something that seem simple bit is enormously important. They help us keep track of day and night which monitors the circadian rhythm that affects our physical, mental, and behavioral changes. This might be one of the greatest contributors to human health because it causes us to get some sleep. Getting adequate sleep is the single most important thing that we do to keep our bodies healthy.

Time and Calendar. The sun and moon were used to create calendars. Some of the earliest calendars were lunar, meaning based on the phases of the moon. The Gregorian calendar that most of the world uses today is solar, based on the sun. Indeed, the Bible, in Genesis chapter one, records that amongst the things that the Creator made during creation week were the sun, moon and stars. He made them on the fourth day (Genesis 1:14-19). The Creator specified that the purpose of these luminous objects was to give light to Earth, to set a clear distinction between night and day, and to indicate signs, seasons, days, and years. Hence, we have used measuring tools such as sundials, clocks, calendars, and almanacs that have enriched, not only our vocabulary, but also our lives.

Community Social. Prior to the advent of electricity, people looked forward to the full moon when they would gather under the moonlight and sing, dance, play games and tell stories; thus, passing on information about their culture and history.

Beauty and the Rainbow. Who does not look up and admire the multicolored rainbow? Recorded in many cultures is the story of a great flood and the rainbow that appeared in the sky. The rainbow was to remind the inhabitants of Earth that the Creator would never again destroy it with a flood. The Bible also records the story of the flood (Genesis chapters 6-8 and 9 verses 1-17). The flood happened after the earth had

become so corrupt that the Creator decided to destroy all living things on Planet Earth. However, he created a way of escape for those who would obey him. He commissioned Noah, a
righteous man, to build a big boat called an ark.
Those who entered the ark would be saved form the flood waters. And that was so. The Creator place in the sky that multicolored arch that often appears after a shower of rain. He placed it there as a reminder that he would never again destroy the earth with a flood.

Star of Bethlehem. Over two thousand years ago, the so-called Star of Bethlehem made an appearance in the sky. The star appeared to some wisemen who looked up and followed it to the birthplace of the Messiah, over which it eventually stopped. The wise men, who came from the East, brought the baby gifts of gold, frankincense, and myrrh. Secular history confirms this event as occurring during the reign of the Roman King Herod. Still today, people verify the event by giving gifts to celebrate the birth of the Messiah. Scientists, however, report that there is no known star that fits the description of the Bethlehem star that welcomed the Messiah, Jesus, on his first advent to Earth in human form. That "star" was neither a meteor nor a comet; therefore, some conclude that it might have been a supernatural object, an astronomical phenomenon just for the occasion.
Start of a Nation. Looking up at the sky also played a significant role at the start of the Jewish nation. It

is recorded in the Bible that God called a man named Abram to be the father of the Jews. However, this man, Abram, whose name God later changed to Abraham, was childless. As the conversation continued, God asked Abraham to look up and count the stars. God then promised Abraham that his descendants would be as numerous as the stars. Thousands of stars can be seen by the naked eye on a dark night. Furthermore, aided by the telescope that allow them to peer more closely at the contents of the heavens, astronomers today report that there are billions of stars above us.

Before modern space exploration, people seemed to have considered the heavens to be the firmament, the sun, moon and stars and God's dwelling place above the sky. However, with the advent of the first telescope and later more powerful ones, mankind has a better view of space. Scientist such as Galileo began looking deeper into the heavens. It is reported that Galileo saw mountains and craters on the moon; similarly, he saw Saturn and even the Milky Way.

The Creator allowed philosophers and scientists to foster the curiosity that would take them above the skies. Then he increased their knowledge and ability to explore deeper into the realms above. Scientists were able to see deeper into space with the new Hubble Telescope launched in 1990. Today, the Hubble space telescope sees a new rival in the launch of the James Webb Telescope which is even more powerful than its predecessor.

Space exploration has yielded discoveries and initiated inventions that benefit mankind in multiple ways. From the discovery of vast galaxies to the awareness of even the smallest dust particles, all come with benefits that have impacted our lives tremendously. The following are few of the great benefits of modern space exploration, and they all echo the love of God for mankind.

Communication Tools: The knowledge gleaned from space exploration has helped to create multiple tools that aid in the propagation of the gospel, the redeeming love of God. One such tool is satellites. Communication satellites are used for television, cellphones, and Internet transmissions. Television, phones, and the Internet have the capability of reaching dwellers all around the globe, to deliver the good news of salvation all around the world. To add to the satellites already beaming from space, Elon Musk and Jeff Bezos have plans to launch thousands of satellites into orbit specifically to enable knowledge to reach even the remotest regions on Earth. Hard-to-reach places for missionaries are easily serviced by programs brought in via satellite. Thus, space exploration helps spread the Gospel of salvation. Interestingly, the Bible says this: "And this gospel of the kingdom will be preached in all the world as a witness to all the nations, and then the end will come." (Matthew 24:14) Another prophetic verse answered Daniel the prophet's question regarding the end of time this way: "But you, Daniel, shut up the words, and seal the book until the time of the end; many shall run to and fro, and knowledge shall increase." (Daniel 12:4)

Navigation Tools: Navigational satellites, such as the Global Positioning System (GPS) aid in calculating exact locations and in managing travel time. Weather satellites are also useful as they forecast weather conditions that might influence functions to spread the good news of salvation. Now people everywhere can more readily find out about their Creator and how much he cares.

Instruction Tools: Space discoveries help us to better understand and appreciate the fact that Earth was especially created habitable for humans, other creatures, and plants that occupy the planet. When we compare the conditions on Earth to that of other planets, or explored locations in the universe, one cannot help but appreciate the depth of thoughts and work that were invested into forming Earth.

Revealing the Creator: Discovering and learning about other worlds in the universe serve as a reminder of God's supremacy and ownership. Astronomical satellites have provided spectacular images of Earth from space along with its solar community. So, we can better appreciate the size, shape, and beauty of our planet home. In addition, the sharp lenses of the Hubble Space Telescope have revealed the presence of distant stars and galaxies, so abundant that scientists are now considering the existence of multiple universes. One cannot deny that the creation of the universe, with all its intricate details, is beyond human comprehension. There must be a supreme being who owns this vast real estate.

Many people understand **look up** and **lift up your heads** to mean that Jesus would be returning soon, and we would all look up and see him when he appears in the sky. However, I believe that Jesus was also admonishing us all to be wise and observe the heavens, the skies, for signs of his second
Additionally, in the same prophetic conversation, Jesus asked his followers **to look up** and **lift up their heads**. "Look up" means the same as "lift up your heads." Why does Jesus repeat himself? From other incidences recorded in the Bible we notice that Jesus repeats himself to place some emphasis of vital importance on his utterances.

Nugget 9:

Modern space exploration has given so much to mankind that it is a challenge to keep up with its giving. In what ways do you benefit from space exploration?

Chapter Ten

Manhattanhenge

Twice per year, the sun sets on the Manhattan Street grids running east to west, aligning itself precisely between the tall buildings, just as if it were taking a sneak peek up the three-mile stretch of 42nd street. It lingers a few minutes, reflecting the splendor of its golden beauty, and then, it moves gracefully along.

It was Dr. Neil DeGrasse Tyson, head of the Hayden Planetarium in New York, who sought out the phenomenon and observed it at the location. Additionally, he coined the word *Manhattanhenge* to name it. The word Manhattanhenge has even been added to the Oxford English dictionary. As a child

Dr. Tyson had visited Stonehenge, the massive monument with vertical standing stones, located in Wiltshire, England and that influenced his naming of the event.

In 2001, Dr. Tyson took his first picture of Manhattanhenge, which the newspaper published in 2002. Every year he furnishes the date of the imminent phenomenon to the newspaper publishers who release it to the public in a timely manner. To date, tens of thousands of people have looked up and have enjoyed the phenomenon in person. Many more do so virtually every year.

The beauty of Manhattanhenge and the enthusiasm of the spectators, who wait for hours in anticipation of the show, are simply amazing! Upon arrival of the show jubilant applauses and shouts ring out as the spectators celebrate. Some of the words that people use to describe the event are awesome, breathtaking, divine, and even spiritual.

Manhattanhenge reminds me of another impressive occasion, referred to as the second advent or the return of the Messiah. Can you imagine how spectacular it will be at the second coming. The feet of the Messiah, S-o-n of God, will not touch the earth at this advent. Instead, he will appear in grand splendor in the sky with an entourage of holy angels and the sound of trumpets. What a magnificent picture!

Do you remember the shofar or ram's horn trumpet in early Israel? Its principal use was to call the people to assemble. So, when Jesus, Son of God returns, he will call the attention of the inhabitance of earth with loud sounding trumpets. His return will not be a silent or secret event. There will be spectators, not only tens of thousands but every living being upon Earth! Revelation 1:7 says that "every eye" shall see him. Every living creature on the earth will know that the Messiah has arrived and look up.

The purpose of his return will be to gather all his faithful people, from Adam time to the time of his return. That will be all who love him and keep his rules. The Bible says that the righteous dead will be raise from the graves, and then, they together with the righteous living will defy gravity as both groups will all be lifted into the sky, up to where King Jesus and his entourage will be hovering.

What will happen to the unrighteous dead and the unrighteous living? The unrighteous dead will remain in their graves; they will not be resurrected. The unrighteous living who witnessed Jesus's return will not withstand the splendor glare or beauty of his righteousness. Thus, they will fall dead. The priestly blessing contains the following: *"The Lord bless you and keep you; The Lord make his face to shine upon you, And be gracious to you, The Lord lift up his countenance upon you And give you peace."* *(Numbers 6:24-26).* The countenance of the Lord Jesus will bless the righteous, but not the unrighteous. The reflection of the Son of God will be too much for the unrighteous to bear.

Jesus and the righteous will all soar away deeper

into space to the place where Jesus has prepared for his righteous followers. And just in case, someone is skeptical of people soaring up into the heavens without assistance of a machine, Jesus defied gravity before when, over two thousand years ago, his
disciples witnessed him return to heaven lifted in a cloud

After Jesus returns with his chosen people, only beings left alive on earth then will be Satan and his evil angels. These will not be able to escape Earth's atmosphere, anymore. They will have no one to tempt. So, they will be bound on the earth until Jesus calls the unrighteousness to face the verdict of the judgment, to pay for their disobedience.

Unlike Manhattanhenge no one knows the date or time of Jesus's return. However, the Bible provides signs that indicate when his coming is fast approaching and one of these signs is space travel.

When I watch the video of Manhattanhenge, I cannot help but think of how spectacle the return of Jesus the Messiah, Lord of the universe will be. It will be unlike anything humans have ever seen before!

Nugget 10:

Have you ever gone to Manhattanhenge? What other lessons we can learn from Manhattanhenge?

Chapter Eleven

Revelation's Happy Ending

Have you noticed that people are getting enthusiastic about leaving Earth behind and setting off to another location in the universe? By whatever means they plan to get there, they are anxiously preparing for lift off, and brilliant minds are working to make it a reality. Up, up, way beyond the sky! How marvelous!

For some, this urge to leave Earth seems to have started with scientist Stephen Hawkins and his battle cry for humans to "hurry" to prepare another home for themselves to avoid Earth's impending doom. Notice the emphasis on the word *hurry*. There now seems to be a race to colonize Mars in a few years

Melinda Ferrari

and make life sustainable beyond Earth

Looking at the elaborate plans and enormous machinery that scientists and engineers have designed to move humanity off planet Earth is mindboggling. Even more astonishing is that humans think they can terraform Mars. How long can a human being live outside of Earth's gravity and still be healthy enough to try to terraform a planet?

Besides worsening conditions predicted on Earth, another reason for people's fears is the prophecy in Revelation. In general, people associate the Book of Revelation in the Bible with complete destruction of the world. The book is believed to contain the prophecy of the apocalypse. However, people seem to overlook the subtitle that reads 'the Revelation of Jesus Christ; consequently, many fear the book and are sacred to even open it, let alone read it.

Revelation reveals the fulfilment of the beautiful work that Jesus has accomplished for human beings. This fulfilment occurs at his second coming. Before Jesus went back to heaven, he had told all his disciples and followers to prepare and watch for his second advent. Revelation is a reminder that Jesus's second advent is fast approaching.

Ironically, once a year the world remembers the first advent of the Messiah, make grand preparations, and then celebrate in the most spectacular way that they can. People celebrate the birth of Jesus by singing joyful songs and giving gifts to one another, yet they shun his revelation. The world seems to be stuck in time, still basking in the first advent while refusing to read about or even prepare for the second advent.

At his first advent, Jesus received gifts of gold, frankincense, and myrrh; however, at his second advent he gives gifts or rewards to everyone on Earth; eternal life, or eternal damnation. Those who receive eternal life will be happy. The heavenly court is presently judging all the Earth's inhabitants, both those who have passed away and those who are alive, and he will reward everyone according to his work. These words are recorded in the Bible. "The Lord looks from heaven. He sees all the sons of men. From the place of His dwelling, He looks He considers all their words." (Psalm 33:13, 14). Another verse, Revelation 22:12 explains that Jesus will return with rewards. It is therefore understandable that before he gets back into Earth's orbit, he will have already decided which reward each person will receive.

Do we know who will receive eternal life? A human being has only a partial knowledge of the character of his fellowmen. It takes the All-knowing, Omnipresent Being who can read deep inside the minds of people and who can see all their actions, to judge accurately. Jesus called the scribes and Pharisees hypocrites because they seemed to fulfill all the requirements of a righteous person, yet they were lawless. He said that they were like whitewashed sepulchers, that looked good on the outside but on the inside, they contained dead bones. You see, some individuals are expert at pretending to be righteous, shiny, and beautiful while their lives are full of dirt.

Even a prophet can be mistaken when he sees through his own eyes. For example, when the prophet Samuel when to anoint the successor to King Saul, he looked at Eliab, son of Jessie, and thought he was perfect for the job. However, the All-knowing, Omnipresent corrected him.

"Do not look at is appearance, or his physical stature, because I have refused him,

For the Lord does not see as man sees,

For man looks at the outward appearance,

but the Lord looks at the heart." (1 Samuel 16: 7, 8).

The Creator has knowledge of all our thoughts, words, actions and even our secrets. He knows our intentions. He is the only being who can truly make someone a saint. Appearance does not count in God's judgement. It is the actual truth that matters. Isaiah chapter 11 mentions a judge who does not rely neither on human eyewitnesses nor earwitnesses to decide a case. God is this Righteous Judge, and he is presently deciding the case of everyone on Earth. When this judgement session has concluded he will reward every person who ever lived on Earth according to his or her work. Proverbs reminds us thus: "The eyes of the Lord see in every place, Keeping watch on the evil and the good." (Proverbs 15:3).

It is evident that the Revelation carries some somber messages. The good news about them is that they are messages of warnings and of hope. The positive side of a warning is that one can heed it and thereby avoid any calamity. Warnings come to protect us. For instance, a warning sign that reads **wet floor** can help people avoid slipping, falling, and hurting themselves. The messages in Revelation have been written for centuries, long enough for everyone to be forewarned and take action to avoid any calamity. This indicates that the Giver of the message, Jesus, cares about us and wants all the inhabitants of Earth to receive eternal life. He wants us to be happy.

Jesus says, "Blessed are those who do his commandments, that they may have the right to the tree of life and may enter through the gates into the city." (Revelation 22:7) The very first chapter the book declares that those who hear and observe the warnings and messages will be happy. I will attempt to create a list of some things Revelation warns about, and later, give the all-in-one remedy to avoid all the calamities.

In general, the principal warnings in the Book of Revelation are against those who disobey God's laws and dishonor him, the Creator of heaven and Earth.

Warnings

The principal warnings can be paraphrased as follows:
   a. Disobeying God's laws will bring destruction.
   b. Dishonoring the Creator of heaven and Earth brings condemnation.

c. Avoid lukewarmness. The result is negative.
d. Do not persecute God's people, you will be severely punished.
e. , Repent from sin! God's wrath will be poured out on sinners.
f. Plagues will be poured out on those who worship other gods.
g. Separate yourself form evil doers and those who will lead you into idolatry.
h. Those who lead people astray will be rejected by God.
i. Do not be deceived by false prophets or false doctrine.
j. All evil doers will be punished.
k. Judgment day has come.
l. Keeping God's laws is required to be chosen for eternal life
m. Obey God, not another human being.

It also gives specific warnings about a beast, an entity to which the dragon or the devil will give power. This evil power, disguised as good, will cause the beast to lead people astray, that is, away from God, causing many to do the wrong thing. This might be the scary part of Revelation because people want to know the identity of beast, that seems to be lurking in the darkness.

Revelation does not only give us warnings, but it also explains how to be on the winning side of the judgment. By heeding the warnings, one will avoid the snares of the beast. If we diligently study our

Bible and follow God's ways, not man's invention, there is no need to be afraid. Revelation gives this solution: "Fear God and give glory to Him, for the hour of His judgment has come; and worship Him who made heaven and earth, the sea and springs of water." (Revelation 14:7)

Scientist Stephen Hawking, an English theoretical physicist, cosmologist, and author remarked that the end will come when the earth turns into a giant fireball. Later in his final work, "A Smooth Exit from Eternal Inflation" he said that the world would end by fading to darkness as the stars run out of energy. (Kharpal,2017)

Judgment Part 1

Well, this is how the Bible explains it. The first part of the judgement happens before Jesus returns. This is when Jesus decides the fate of all the inhabitants who ever lived on Earth, both the living and the dead who are in the graves. On the day of his return, the first part of the judgment will have already ended; that is, the just will already have been found righteous and the unjust, unrighteous. The righteous ones are those who accept Jesus as their savior and keep his laws, before the day of his arrival.

Judgment Part 2

When Jesus comes to give his rewards, it is the second phase of the judgement. He already knows who will receive what reward. The righteous, will inherit eternal life and the unrighteous damnation. The sound of the trumpet will cause the righteous dead to resurrect and be transformed into their new body. They and the righteous living, who will also be transformed, will fly up into the air to where Jesus is. They include both the righteous dead from Adam to the coming of the Messiah and the righteous living at the time of his arrival

The unrighteous dead will not be resurrected at this time and the unrighteous living, not being able to withstand the righteousness of the King Jesus, will all fall dead. So, the earth will be desolate leaving only the dead, Satan, and his evil angels on it.

The Righteous on Vacation

The righteous people redeemed from the earth will travel through space, without the use of any machinery, to the place that Jesus had told his disciples 2000 years ago that he would go prepare for the saints. Revelation also gives a beautiful picture of the people who will be granted salvation. All will participate in a grand celebration above the skies. There will be playing of instruments and rejoicing, singing of songs, and giving praises and thanks. Can you imagine meeting up again with your loved one who have passed away! Can you imagine meeting Adam, Eve, Abraham, Elijah, Moses, and other patriarchs in person! That will be a grand reunion and a awesome celebration!

Judgment Part 3

According to the Book of Revelation, the righteous will spend a thousand years in heaven. Besides meeting greeting and rejoicing, another thing that the righteous will do in heaven is to review the records of the lives of those who were not saved form the earth. Indeed, God will open the book so that every saint can see the reason the lost are lost!

After the 1000 years in heaven, Jesus and the righteous, the saved people, return to the space above Earth, on the city called New Jerusalem, for the third and final phase of the judgement. As the city hovers over the earth, all the unrighteous are resurrected to face their judgement along with Satan and his evil angels. Consequently, all evil is wiped off the face of the earth, by fire and brimstone, never to return.

New Earth

After the earth is cleansed of sin, God creates a new earth with New Jerusalem as its capital. Some of the blessings of living in the new earth are as follows:

    a. There will be no more death, sorrow, pain, or suffering.

    b. No one will be ever tired or bored.

    c. Envy, jealousy, murder, and all evil will become extinct.

    d. All the animals will be tame.

    e. The saints will enjoy beauties beyond the imagination of any human mind.

f. All will learn more about God's love for mankind.
g. Everyone will worship God face-to-face.
h. All will visit with family, friends, and ancient patriarch.
i. We will travel with Jesus.
j. The saints will sing victory songs and play musical instruments.
k. God will sing over us.
l. God will set up his headquarters on the new earth.

When Will Jesus Arrive?

The big question is, when will this be? The Book of Daniel gives us this striking clue. "But you, Daniel, shut up the words, and seal the book until the time of the end; many shall run to and fro, and knowledge shall increase." (Daniel 12: 4).

As you read the verse above, realize that the angel had come from up in the heavens down to Earth, back and forth, and as he explained, when men started traveling *to and fro,* meaning likewise, the end would come. Observing current events, anyone can realize that we are living in the time of the end. Space tourism has become a reality; people are traveling to space and back.

We may ask when the exact date of the end will be, however, only the Creator knows that. Jesus himself, while he was on Earth, explained to the disciples that no one knows this time but the Father in heaven.

The Creator himself instituted the concept of time. He started dividing day and night from the very first day of creation. He works in conjunction with time and the time for man's redemption is on his schedule. The Book of Revelation gives us insights into God's schedule. He wants us to know when the time is near. How wonderful!

In conclusion, the final victory will be for those who heed God's warnings and wisely choose to follow his ways. They did not rely on the words of others. With the help of the Holy Spirit, they research the facts and concluded as did King Solomon that men ought to "fear God and keep his commandments." (Ecclesiastes12:13) Furthermore, "The wise shall inherit glory, But shame shall be the legacy of fools." *(Proverbs 3:35)*

Nugget 11:

Does the Creator know the names of everyone who ever lived on Earth? Of what material do you think the record books will be made? Learn more.

Chapter Twelve

Space Sounds

According to National Aeronautics and Space Administration (NASA), space is a vacuum, and a vacuum does not allow sound to pass through it. Therefore, humans are not able to hear sounds in space where there is emptiness between stars and planets. Sound needs a medium such as air or water through which to pass so we can hear it. Since there is no material for sound to travel through in empty space, no sound is heard there.

However, various types of waves such as radio waves, gravitational waves and magnetic waves are present, and these can travel without a medium.

Based on this information, NASA has devised ways to capture these waves and convert them into sounds.

NASA sent out probes such as the Voyager, and on these probes, they placed instruments capable of capturing and recording sound waves. Back on Earth, the waves are translated into sounds that humans can appreciate.

What strikes me most is that at this time in Earth's history people have developed an interest in listening to sounds from above the skies. To me, this is fascinating because prophecy reveals that we are living in the time of Earth's history when mankind will soon hear a special sound coming from above.

Sound of the trumpets.

I am amazed that scientists are so interested in sounds from space because not long from now, there will be some mighty sounds coming from the heavens above. These sounds will be so piercing that even the deaf will hear them! Earth's activities will all come to a sudden stop. The attention of all will be focused on the grand finale of the galactic sound of angels sounding trumpets as the Messiah, King of kings, rides in, high upon the clouds. He rides across the galaxies between interstellar space accompanied by an entourage of angels playing loud sounding trumpets. The earth will shake, causing islands to disappear from their places. It is the year of the jubilee, and the King comes to release his people from bondage.

We do not know whether the Messiah will come within Earth's lower orbit, middle orbit, or hover in the geostationary orbit. However, we know, as per the Bible that everyone will see him immediately and that his feet will not touch the ground (1 Thessalonians 4:17). His glories will beam from the heavens and every inhabitant of the earth will be immediately affected by it, even those who despise him.

The trumpet call is not a strange arrangement for God to use to gather his people. While the Israelites were traveling through the wilderness to the Promised Land, God instructed Moses to make two silver trumpets. The sons of Aaron the priests were responsible for blowing the trumpet. The main purpose of the silver trumpets was for the gathering of the people, for assembly or to continue their journey. It is understandable then that God would use the same pattern to call the world to attention when he comes to gather his people to take them to the place, he has prepared for them.

The glorious appearance of Jesus will fill some with joy and others with fear. Mighty men will be shaken to the core like babies. Those who are prepared to meet the King will shout will joyfully sounds of praise. Fear and the light of God's righteousness countenance will cause the guilty to fall dead, but dead saints to resurrect from their graves and fly up, together with the righteous living, to greet the Redeemer in the air.

Sound of the Harps

Another instrument mentioned in Revelation is the harp. It is associated with worship, victory, and praise. Above all, it is an instrument that symbolizes healing. So, the end of time on Earth will be the beginning of rejoicing in the cosmos for God's people. The redeemed from the Earth will play harps and rejoice for having been victorious over the evil one.

It is interesting to note that, according to the Bible, the first instrument that was invented was the harp, and now we understand that the last instrument to be used will be the harp. We also know that it was Jubal, the eighth generation of Cain, who invented the harp. Even though Cain had committed an awful crime and had been banished from God's presence, God had mercy and gave this wonderful gift of invention to one of his descendants. So, God caused some joy to spring forth from Cain's sorrowful situation. Thus, the Creator highlighted his arms of mercy that are open to anyone who will accept his embrace.

The harp was a staple in ancient Israel, and it played a prominent part in worship and in the emotional stability of the people. When the people were captives in another land, their sadness prevented them from playing their harp, the instrument of praise that brought them much happiness. As Psalm 137 explains, instead of playing, they hung their harps upon willow trees.

The harp played a significant role in worship in biblical times. The works of King David, the most prolific harpist in the Bible, makes the harp familiar to even those who have never seen one in person. Many people know the story of David playing the harp for King Saul who was troubled by an evil spirit. When David played for Saul, the music calmed his disturbed spirit, and he became well again.

Furthermore, during the latter years of King David's reign, he assigned, two hundred and eighty-eight temple musicians, many of whom played the harp and prophesied upon it. Likewise, the redeemed from the earth will praise God in triumph upon the harp as they lift their voices in joyful praise.

Sound of Rejoicing

Revelation chapter 15 tells us that the triumphal saints will sing the song of Moses and the Lamb. The redeemed from all nations will praise God for his mighty acts and his righteousness as they play their harps. The song of Moses and the Lamb is a song of triumph. Moses, with the help of the Almighty was successful in leading the children of Israel across the Red Sea, leaving behind the enemies who pursued them. Exodus chapter 15 tells us how Moses led the people in praise to God after they had all crossed over the Red Sea and were safe on the other side. Moses also, with God's help, triumphed over the accusations of Satan who appeared at his resurrection and tried to prevent it. However, according to Jude

1:9, Michael the archangel rebuked the devil and raised Moses to eternal life.

Jesus, the Lamb, came to Earth and accomplished his mission of securing our salvation. He triumphed over sin and that joyful occasion made our redemption possible. Likewise, the saints will rejoice in heaven having overcome the enemy.

Soon, the cosmos will ring out with the mighty sounds of trumpets for everyone to hear with their own ears. Life on Earth will end with that angelic grand finale of trumpets. Later, a new life in heaven, a vacation of a thousand years, begins with the exuberant prelude of rejoicing as the redeemed play harps and sing the song of Moses and the Lamb and the heavens resound with hallelujahs!

Nugget 12:

Is it by mere chance that the inhabitants of Earth have started listening for sounds in the cosmos?

Conclusion

It appears that the Creator of the universe is using multiple space discoveries simultaneously to alert the inhabitants of Earth that something special is about to happen. It seems evident that phenomenal events are approaching, and nature above has invited us to behold its pages and learn.

Fortunately, this generation has received ample warnings and instructions to be knowledgeable about end-time challenges. Will we exercise wisdom and respond appropriately?

Space discoveries have prophesied to us and will continue to do so until the end of time as we know it. What we do with the information could help determine our fate.

Melinda Ferrari

About The Author

Melinda Ferrari has over 35 years of experience teaching students from pre-kindergarten through adult education. She has taught students from different continents, linguistic backgrounds, and cultures.

Melinda is a schoolteacher, specializing in K-12 Bilingual Education (English/Spanish) and Elementary Education. She is also a musician who has provided organ and piano music for several Christian congregations since she was a teenager. In addition, she is a student at heart and continues to drink from the vast reservoir of knowledge in the universe.

Melinda Ferrari

Bibliography

Chiao L. (March 3, 2016) Return to Earth: An Astronaut's view of coming home. https://www.space.com/32102-astronaut-perspective-on-long-deployments.html

Crookes, D. (2022) Roswell incident: The truth behind the "flying saucer" crash https://space.com/the-truth-about/what-is-the-truth-behind-the-roswell-ufo-incident

Kharpal A. (May 5, 2017) Stephen Hawking says humans must colonize another planet in 100 years or face extinction.

https://www.cnbc.com/2017/05/05/stephen-hawking-human-extinction-colonize-planet.html

National Geographics (n. d) The History of Space Exploration https://education.nationalgeographic.org/resource/history-space-exploration

Nasa Science (n.d.) Solar System Exploration https://solarsystem.nasa.gov/planets/overview

Tyson, N (Host), (2015-present) Star Talk (Video

podcast) https://startalkmedia.com

www.ingramcontent.com/pod-product-compliance
Lightning Source LLC
Chambersburg PA
CBHW072235290326
41934CB00008BA/1310